PRINCEWILL LAGANG

Rediscovering Romance

First published by PRINCEWILL LAGANG 2023

Copyright © 2023 by Princewill Lagang

All rights reserved. No part of this publication may be reproduced, stored or transmitted in any form or by any means, electronic, mechanical, photocopying, recording, scanning, or otherwise without written permission from the publisher. It is illegal to copy this book, post it to a website, or distribute it by any other means without permission.

Princewill Lagang asserts the moral right to be identified as the author of this work.

First edition

This book was professionally typeset on Reedsy.
Find out more at reedsy.com

Contents

1	Rediscovering Romance in Relationships	1
2	The Changing Landscape of Love	3
3	The Power of Mindful Partnership	6
4	Reconnecting Through Communication	9
5	The Art of Surprise and Spontaneity	12
6	Recapturing Intimacy	15
7	Exploring New Experiences Together	19
8	Rekindling Passion	22
9	Reimagining Date Nights	25
10	Overcoming Routine and Stress	29
11	Rediscovering Self and Partner	33
12	Sustaining a Lifelong Journey of Romance	37

1

Rediscovering Romance in Relationships

In a world bustling with fast-paced routines and digital distractions, the tender flame of romance often finds itself flickering in the shadows of everyday life. This book embarks on a transformative journey, delving into the art of reigniting passion and rediscovering the magic of connection within relationships.

As we flip through the pages of our lives, we often stumble upon a chapter titled "Romance" that might have lost its luster over time. We might find ourselves reminiscing about the early days of our relationships when every glance held a secret, every touch carried a promise, and every word was poetry. The sensation of being in love was an intoxicating elixir that colored our world with hues of enchantment.

However, it's not uncommon for couples to experience a gradual fading of this enchantment as the years roll on. The responsibilities of careers, raising families, and maintaining households can inadvertently cast a shadow over the flames that once burned brightly. The familiarity of daily routines and the weight of commitments often obscure the view of the passionate bond that initially brought two people together.

But here, in these pages, we embark on a journey of rediscovery. A journey that seeks to recapture the essence of those early days, not by erasing the years that have passed, but by infusing them with the same sense of wonder, desire, and connection that once blossomed effortlessly. It's a journey that invites you to rekindle the flame, not as an escape from reality, but as an enhancement of it.

Throughout this book, we'll explore a tapestry of strategies, stories, and insights that unravel the layers of what romance truly means in the context of enduring relationships. We'll discover that romance isn't solely about grand gestures or lavish gifts, but about the small, consistent acts of love and appreciation that create a symphony of affection in everyday life.

Prepare to be captivated by the tales of couples who have rekindled their love amidst the challenges of life. Be ready to dive into the psychology of passion and connection, understanding the factors that influence their ebbs and flows. Together, we'll cultivate a new perspective on intimacy—one that embraces vulnerability, communication, and shared experiences.

So, as you embark on this journey of rediscovery, open your heart to the possibilities that lie ahead. Let these words be your guide as you navigate the terrain of rekindling romance. May the stories shared and the insights unveiled serve as stepping stones on the path to reigniting the spark that has been waiting patiently to be rekindled.

2

The Changing Landscape of Love

Love, like all living entities, evolves with the passage of time. In the early days of a relationship, it's often accompanied by an intoxicating blend of passion, novelty, and excitement. However, as the journey progresses, the landscape of love undergoes a transformation that can challenge even the most enduring bonds. This chapter delves into the evolution of relationships and the challenges that can lead to a decline in romance.

From Infatuation to Intimacy: The Evolution of Love

The initial stage of a relationship is often characterized by infatuation. Every touch sends shivers down the spine, and the mere thought of the other person ignites a rush of excitement. This phase, while exhilarating, is also fleeting. As time passes, the relationship transitions from this intense infatuation to a deeper stage of intimacy. While the fiery passion of the early days may not burn as brightly, it is replaced by a sense of familiarity, comfort, and emotional closeness that forms the foundation of enduring love.

The Challenges that Erode Romance

However, with the evolution of a relationship come challenges that can gradually erode the romance that once thrived. One of the primary culprits is the growing presence of responsibilities and commitments. The demands of careers, parenting, and managing household affairs can divert attention and energy away from nurturing the romantic connection. As partners become engrossed in their individual roles, they may find themselves neglecting the effort required to keep the flame of romance alive.

Communication breakdowns also contribute to the decline of romance. As partners become more comfortable with each other, assumptions about desires and feelings can replace open dialogue. Unaddressed concerns or unspoken expectations can create a chasm between partners, leading to emotional distance and a lack of intimacy.

Furthermore, routine and predictability can dampen the sparks of passion. The absence of novelty in everyday interactions can make partners feel like they're trapped in a monotonous cycle, stifling the excitement that once characterized their relationship.

Nurturing Romance in the Midst of Change

Acknowledging the changing landscape of love is the first step toward rekindling romance. Couples must recognize that the evolution of their relationship is natural and doesn't signify a loss of love. Instead, it's an opportunity to deepen their connection through shared experiences, understanding, and adaptability.

Efforts to combat the challenges must involve intentional actions. Carving out quality time for each other, even amid busy schedules, can be revitalizing. Engaging in new activities together and creating opportunities for surprises can inject a dose of excitement into the relationship. Moreover, prioritizing open communication and addressing concerns promptly can prevent the growth of emotional distance.

In essence, understanding that love transforms doesn't mean resigning to its decline. It means embracing the evolution and actively participating in nurturing the flame that keeps a relationship alive. As we journey through this chapter, let's not only recognize the changes that love undergoes but also explore the ways in which we can embrace them to cultivate a more profound and enduring romance.

3

The Power of Mindful Partnership

In a world marked by constant distractions and the incessant pull of technology, the art of mindful partnership emerges as a cornerstone in the journey of rekindling romance. This chapter explores the significance of being present and attentive to your partner, offering techniques to cultivate mindfulness and enrich the quality of your relationship.

The Present Gift of Presence

Imagine a moment when you're truly present with your partner: eyes locked, hearts engaged, and the outside world fades into insignificance. This state of mindful presence is a gift you give not only to your partner but also to yourself. It's the antidote to the hurriedness of life that can often relegate relationships to the periphery.

When you're mindful in your partnership, you actively engage in the moments you share. You listen with intention, communicate with authenticity, and immerse yourself in the depth of the connection you're nurturing. This presence not only fosters a sense of emotional closeness but also allows you to truly experience and appreciate the nuances of your partner's presence.

Cultivating Mindfulness in Partnership

1. Practice Active Listening: When your partner speaks, listen not just to respond but to understand. Put aside distractions, maintain eye contact, and give your full attention. This simple act communicates respect and validates your partner's feelings.

2. Mindful Communication: Before reacting, take a breath. Allow space for your thoughts and emotions to settle before responding. This prevents knee-jerk reactions that can escalate conflicts and create emotional distance.

3. Technology-Free Time: Dedicate specific periods of time to disconnect from technology and connect with each other. This could be a daily walk, a weekly date night, or a device-free hour before bed.

4. Gratitude and Appreciation: Express genuine appreciation for your partner regularly. Acknowledge the efforts they put into the relationship and the qualities you admire. This cultivates a positive atmosphere of love and respect.

5. Shared Experiences: Engage in activities that encourage joint participation and shared experiences. It could be cooking a meal together, taking a dance class, or embarking on a new hobby. These experiences create lasting memories and provide opportunities for bonding.

6. Mindful Touch: Physical touch is a powerful way to convey love and connection. Be mindful of the touch you share—hold hands, hug, and kiss with intention, allowing the warmth of your affection to be felt deeply.

7. Gratitude Journaling: Maintain a journal in which you both write down things you're grateful for in each other and your relationship. This practice shifts the focus from what's lacking to what's abundant.

The Ripple Effect of Mindful Partnership

Practicing mindfulness in your partnership extends beyond the immediate connection between you and your partner. It ripples outward, positively influencing the overall atmosphere of your relationship. As you cultivate mindfulness, you create an environment of emotional safety and understanding. You offer your partner the space to be vulnerable, knowing that their thoughts and feelings are valued and heard.

The power of mindful partnership is that it transforms ordinary moments into extraordinary connections. It turns routine interactions into meaningful exchanges, fostering an enduring sense of intimacy. As you journey through this chapter, embrace the practice of being present with your partner and witness how this mindful approach enriches the tapestry of your love story.

4

Reconnecting Through Communication

Effective communication serves as the bridge that reconnects hearts, reigniting the spark of romance that may have dimmed over time. This chapter delves into the pivotal role of communication in revitalizing relationships, offering strategies to deepen conversations and embrace the art of active listening.

The Language of Connection

Communication is not just about words; it's about the unspoken emotions, the nuances of tone, and the subtle gestures that convey meaning. When partners communicate openly and authentically, they create a space where they can be themselves without fear of judgment or misunderstanding. This open dialogue becomes the canvas upon which the portrait of their romance is painted.

Strategies for Deepening Conversations

1. Create Conversation Rituals: Set aside specific times for meaningful conversations. It could be over morning coffee or during evening walks.

These designated times foster anticipation and provide a platform for sharing thoughts and feelings.

2. Share Dreams and Aspirations: Encourage each other to share dreams, both big and small. Discuss goals you want to achieve individually and as a couple. This creates a sense of unity and mutual support.

3. Practice Vulnerability: Open up about your fears, insecurities, and struggles. Vulnerability invites empathy and nurtures a deeper connection as you share your inner world with your partner.

4. Ask Open-Ended Questions: Instead of asking yes-or-no questions, ask questions that prompt detailed responses. For instance, replace "Did you have a good day?" with "Tell me about your day. What stood out to you?"

5. Reflective Listening: After your partner speaks, paraphrase what they've said to ensure you've understood correctly. This shows that you're engaged and willing to comprehend their perspective.

The Art of Active Listening

Active listening goes beyond merely hearing words—it's about fully engaging with your partner's thoughts and emotions. When you practice active listening, you communicate that their words matter and that you're genuinely interested in their experiences.

1. Eliminate Distractions: Put away phones, turn off the TV, and create an environment conducive to focused conversation.

2. Maintain Eye Contact: Eye contact shows that you're attentive and emotionally present in the conversation.

3. Nonverbal Cues: Nodding, smiling, and using facial expressions to reflect

understanding and empathy can reinforce your engagement.

4. Resist Interrupting: Allow your partner to finish their thoughts before responding. Interrupting can derail the flow of the conversation and make your partner feel unheard.

5. Empathize: Put yourself in your partner's shoes and try to understand their feelings and perspective. This creates a bond of empathy and emotional connection.

The Resurgence of Romance through Communication

As partners become adept at deepening conversations and practicing active listening, they create a fertile ground for the rekindling of romance. Sharing thoughts, emotions, and dreams allows partners to see each other with fresh eyes and appreciate the evolving depth of their relationship. The trust that blossoms from open and empathetic communication forms a sturdy foundation upon which love can thrive.

Through the pages of this chapter, embrace communication as the tool that breathes life back into your relationship. As you engage in conversations that are genuine, deep, and heart-centered, you'll find that the flame of romance burns brighter, illuminating the path toward a reinvigorated and enduring connection.

5

The Art of Surprise and Spontaneity

In the tapestry of a relationship, surprises and spontaneity are the vibrant threads that weave moments of joy, excitement, and connection. This chapter celebrates the magic of unexpected gestures and unplanned experiences, guiding you through the journey of rediscovering the joy that comes with infusing surprise and spontaneity into your relationship.

The Enchantment of Surprises

Remember the flutter of excitement that accompanied a surprise birthday party or an unexpected gift? Surprises have a remarkable ability to evoke emotions that linger in our memories. They serve as reminders that we are cherished and that our partners go the extra mile to see us smile. In relationships, surprises hold the potential to rekindle the spark by injecting an element of excitement and novelty.

Unplanned Moments of Spontaneity

Spontaneity is the antidote to routine. It's the impulse to seize the moment and embark on an adventure without a predefined script. Spontaneous acts inject life into the everyday, fostering a sense of playfulness and vibrancy that can wane in the face of responsibilities.

Ideas for Injecting Spontaneity

1. Impromptu Getaways: Plan a spontaneous day trip to a nearby town or a weekend escape to a charming bed-and-breakfast.

2. Cooking Adventures: Choose a recipe you've never tried before and cook a surprise dinner for your partner.

3. Random Acts of Kindness: Leave surprise notes or small gifts in unexpected places for your partner to discover throughout the day.

4. Dance Party: Transform the living room into a dance floor and have an impromptu dance party to your favorite songs.

5. Stargazing: Set up a cozy spot in the backyard for stargazing and enjoying each other's company under the night sky.

6. Tech-Free Day: Declare a tech-free day where you both disconnect from screens and enjoy quality time together.

The Gateway to Connection

Surprises and spontaneity are not about grand gestures; they're about injecting a sense of wonder into everyday life. They communicate thoughtfulness, ignite laughter, and inspire a renewed sense of appreciation. When partners engage in these acts, they communicate that their love is alive, evolving, and dedicated to nurturing the spirit of their relationship.

Cultivating a Culture of Surprise and Spontaneity

Creating a culture of surprise and spontaneity requires a willingness to step outside of comfort zones and embrace the unexpected. Partners can set aside time to brainstorm ideas together, ensuring that surprises align with each other's preferences and values. Remember, the goal is not perfection, but the genuine intent to make each other feel cherished and celebrated.

As you explore the pages of this chapter, let the concept of surprise and spontaneity become an integral part of your relationship's narrative. By infusing moments with unexpected joy and embracing unplanned adventures, you'll rediscover the exhilaration of living in the moment and sharing in the delight of love's vibrant tapestry.

6

Recapturing Intimacy

Intimacy is the sacred realm where emotional connection and physical closeness intertwine, breathing life into the heart of a relationship. This chapter delves into the profound significance of nurturing both emotional and physical intimacy, providing insights into overcoming barriers and reigniting desire to recapture the rich tapestry of closeness and passion.

Embracing Emotional Intimacy

Emotional intimacy forms the foundation upon which a strong relationship is built. It's about sharing vulnerabilities, fears, hopes, and dreams—revealing your innermost self to your partner. When partners foster emotional intimacy, they create a safe space where their true selves can flourish without judgment.

Nurturing Emotional Intimacy:

1. Open Communication: Encourage honest conversations about thoughts, feelings, and experiences, even if they're difficult to share.

2. Active Listening: Listen with empathy and without interruption, showing that your partner's emotions are valued and respected.

3. Supportive Environment: Create an atmosphere where both partners feel comfortable expressing themselves without fear of criticism.

Rediscovering Physical Intimacy

Physical intimacy is the bridge between emotional connection and passionate desire. It's not merely about sexual acts but the profound closeness that comes from touch, closeness, and shared experiences. As relationships evolve, physical intimacy requires conscious effort to reignite and sustain.

Reigniting Physical Intimacy:

1. Prioritize Touch: Initiate physical touch throughout the day, whether it's a hug, a kiss, or holding hands. Physical contact fosters a sense of connection.

2. Quality Time: Dedicate uninterrupted moments to each other, where you can engage in activities that promote closeness and bonding.

3. Exploration and Adventure: Try new experiences together that can spark excitement and ignite a sense of shared adventure.

Overcoming Barriers to Intimacy

Barriers to intimacy can arise from various sources, including stress, past experiences, and communication breakdowns. Recognizing these barriers is the first step toward addressing them.

Overcoming Intimacy Barriers:

1. Communication: Address concerns openly, discussing any issues that may

be hindering intimacy.

2. Stress Management: Find healthy ways to manage stress, as excessive stress can impact emotional and physical intimacy.

3. Professional Help: If past experiences or emotional challenges are affecting intimacy, consider seeking guidance from a therapist.

Reigniting Desire

As relationships evolve, desire can sometimes wane due to familiarity or complacency. However, desire can be reignited with intention and effort.

Rekindling Desire:

1. Novelty: Introduce novelty into the relationship, whether it's through new activities or exploring new aspects of each other's personalities.

2. Flirting: Embrace playful teasing, flirty messages, and gestures that remind each other of the initial stages of attraction.

3. Date Nights: Set aside dedicated time for date nights to rekindle the excitement and passion that characterized the early days.

The Path to Recaptured Intimacy

Recapturing intimacy involves a commitment to both emotional vulnerability and physical closeness. Partners must recognize that intimacy is not static; it's an evolving journey that requires nurturing, attention, and adaptability.

Through the exploration of this chapter, let the understanding of emotional and physical intimacy guide your efforts to reignite the passion within your relationship. By embracing the depth of connection that intimacy offers and overcoming barriers that hinder it, you'll embark on a transformative journey toward rediscovering the profound beauty of love in its most intimate form.

7

Exploring New Experiences Together

In the realm of relationships, growth thrives where comfort zones fade. This chapter illuminates the profound impact of stepping outside familiarity as a couple, embracing the magic of trying new activities and embarking on adventures that cultivate shared growth, deepen bonds, and rekindle the flame of connection.

The Magic Beyond Comfort Zones

Comfort zones provide a sense of security, but they can also become stifling over time. When partners dare to venture beyond these boundaries, they open the door to a world of shared experiences that invigorate their connection. New experiences not only enrich life but also inspire personal and relational growth.

Triumphs and Challenges: The Heart of Growth

Every new endeavor comes with its set of triumphs and challenges. The pursuit of shared growth requires partners to embrace the journey, understanding that successes and setbacks contribute to the tapestry of their relationship.

Trying New Activities:

1. Discover Shared Interests: Experiment with activities you've never tried before, discovering new hobbies or interests you can both enjoy.

2. Cultivate Curiosity: Approach new experiences with an open mind and a sense of curiosity, eager to learn and explore together.

3. Celebrate Progress: Celebrate each other's accomplishments, whether big or small. This fosters a sense of mutual support and encouragement.

Embarking on Adventures:

1. Step into the Unknown: Choose adventures that challenge you to step outside your comfort zone, whether it's hiking a challenging trail or traveling to a foreign destination.

2. Shared Goals: Set goals for your adventures, whether it's completing a challenging hike or participating in a charity run. The sense of achievement reinforces your bond.

3. Embrace Flexibility: Understand that not every adventure will unfold as planned. Embrace flexibility and see unexpected turns as part of the experience.

Shared Growth as a Foundation

Trying new activities and embarking on adventures forms the foundation of shared growth. Partners learn more about each other's strengths, weaknesses, and capacities for resilience. The bond forged through these experiences becomes a powerful testament to their ability to navigate challenges together.

Strengthening the Relationship:

1. Communication: Engaging in new experiences opens doors for conversations about desires, fears, and aspirations, enhancing communication.

2. Creating Memories: The memories created through shared experiences become cherished stories that define your journey together.

3. Rekindling Passion: Stepping outside comfort zones injects excitement and novelty into the relationship, reigniting the flames of passion.

Embracing the Journey of Shared Growth

Exploring new experiences together isn't solely about the destination—it's about the journey of discovery, vulnerability, and connection. Partners grow not only individually but also as a unit, bonded by the memories and challenges they've shared.

Through the wisdom within these pages, let the spirit of exploration guide your journey as a couple. As you embrace new activities and embark on adventures, you'll find yourselves weaving a vibrant tapestry of shared growth, creating a legacy of love that continually blossoms with each step you take beyond the boundaries of familiarity.

8

Rekindling Passion

Passion is the heartbeat of a romantic connection, the electric current that courses through the veins of a thriving relationship. This chapter delves into the intricate dance of reigniting desire and maintaining a vibrant sex life, unraveling the factors that contribute to passionate connection and offering techniques to stoke the fires of passion.

The Complex Tapestry of Passion

Passion is a delicate fusion of emotional, physical, and psychological elements that ignite desire and infuse relationships with fervor. It thrives on novelty, emotional closeness, and the freedom to express desires without inhibition.

Understanding Passionate Connection:

1. Novelty and Mystery: Introduce novelty into your relationship to maintain an air of mystery. Novel experiences stimulate the brain's reward centers, sparking desire.

2. Emotional Intimacy: Passion blossoms when partners share emotional

closeness and vulnerability. A strong emotional bond fuels a sense of safety and trust.

3. Desire to Please: Genuine desire to please your partner fosters an atmosphere of mutual care and affection, driving the motivation to ignite passion.

Techniques for Rekindling Desire:

1. Flirtation: Engage in playful teasing and flirtatious behavior, reigniting the playful spark that characterized the early stages of the relationship.

2. Quality Time: Dedicate time to connect on a deep level, creating an environment where both partners feel cherished and desired.

3. Surprise and Spontaneity: Inject surprise and spontaneity into your intimate moments, keeping the anticipation alive.

Maintaining a Vibrant Sex Life:

1. Communication: Have open conversations about desires, fantasies, and preferences, ensuring both partners feel comfortable expressing their needs.

2. Variety: Experiment with new experiences, from trying different locations to exploring sensual techniques that enhance connection.

3. Mutual Exploration: Encourage mutual exploration and experimentation to deepen intimacy and expand the boundaries of pleasure.

Breaking Barriers to Passion:

Barriers to passion can arise from various sources, including stress, body image issues, and past experiences. Recognizing and addressing these barriers is crucial to reigniting desire.

Overcoming Barriers:

1. Stress Management: Prioritize stress reduction techniques, such as mindfulness, exercise, and relaxation, to create a conducive environment for passion.

2. Body Positivity: Cultivate a positive body image by practicing self-love and acceptance, allowing yourself to feel confident and desired.

3. Professional Help: If past experiences or emotional challenges are impacting passion, consider seeking guidance from a therapist.

The Dance of Passion Rekindled

Passion is not a fixed entity—it's a dynamic force that can be rekindled with intention and effort. Partners must acknowledge that maintaining passion requires nurturing, exploration, and a willingness to adapt.

As you journey through this chapter, let the understanding of the factors that contribute to passionate connection guide your efforts. By embracing the techniques that stoke desire and maintaining an atmosphere of openness, you'll embark on a transformative journey toward reigniting the fires of passion, infusing your relationship with an enduring and intoxicating sense of intimacy.

9

Reimagining Date Nights

Date nights are not just mere outings; they're the threads that weave the fabric of connection in a relationship. This chapter elevates the concept of date nights, transforming them into opportunities for profound impact. It explores the art of planning meaningful and memorable experiences as a couple, breathing life into your shared journey of love.

The Power of Intentional Connection

Date nights, when approached with intention, transcend the mundane. They're a chance to reconnect, deepen intimacy, and create lasting memories. Elevating date nights requires a shift from routine outings to purposeful experiences that nurture the heart of your relationship.

Crafting Meaningful Experiences:

1. Themes and Adventures: Infuse creativity into your date nights by choosing themes or embarking on mini-adventures. Themes can range from "Cultural Exploration" to "Romantic Getaway."

2. Surprise Elements: Incorporate surprise elements that your partner wouldn't expect. This could involve hidden love notes, a surprise activity, or revisiting a special place from your past.

3. Shared Goals: Collaborate on a project or a challenge during your date night, fostering a sense of teamwork and collaboration.

Memories That Last a Lifetime

Meaningful date nights create memories that remain etched in your relationship's tapestry. These memories become the cornerstones of shared experiences that you can revisit and cherish.

Planning Memorable Experiences:

1. Thoughtful Details: Pay attention to the details, such as the ambiance, music, and even the attire you choose for the night.

2. New Perspectives: Explore places you've never been before or see familiar locations from a new perspective to add a layer of novelty to your experience.

3. Culinary Adventures: Try new restaurants or cuisines, or cook a special meal together to elevate the dining experience.

Breaking Free from Routine

Routine can inadvertently stifle the sense of novelty in a relationship. Reimagined date nights offer a reprieve from the everyday, invigorating your connection.

Creating Variety:

1. Thematic Diversity: Rotate between different types of date nights, such as

adventurous, romantic, cultural, and intellectual.

2. Scheduled Spontaneity: Surprise your partner with unplanned date nights, infusing spontaneity into your routine.

3. Shared Planning: Alternate in planning date nights, allowing each partner to take turns curating memorable experiences.

The Heartbeat of Reimagined Connection

Reimagining date nights transforms them from routine rituals into moments that celebrate the uniqueness of your relationship. These experiences invite you to explore, connect, and revel in the joy of each other's company.

Creating a Ritual of Connection:

1. Consistency: Dedicate specific days for date nights to create a ritual that you both look forward to.

2. No Distractions: Keep phones and distractions away to ensure that you're fully present and engaged.

3. Reflect and Cherish: After each date night, take a moment to reflect on the experience and express gratitude for your partner's efforts.

Breathing Life into Love

Reimagining date nights transforms them into transformative experiences that nurture the heart of your relationship. By crafting meaningful, memorable moments, you're not only celebrating your shared journey but also nurturing the enduring flame of your love story.

As you journey through this chapter, let the concept of reimagined date nights guide your path. Embrace the art of planning experiences that transcend the ordinary and breathe life into your love, creating a legacy of cherished memories that will continue to bloom with each passing day.

10

Overcoming Routine and Stress

Routine and stress, while inevitable in the tapestry of life, can inadvertently cast a shadow on the vibrant colors of romance. This chapter unveils strategies for navigating the challenges of routine and stress, providing insights into maintaining closeness during busy and demanding times, and ensuring that love continues to flourish despite life's demands.

The Intricacies of Routine and Stress

Routine provides structure, but it can also lead to complacency. Stress, on the other hand, can obscure the beauty of connection. Balancing these elements is pivotal to keeping the flame of romance alive.

Navigating Routine and Stress:

1. Awareness: Recognize when routine and stress are impacting your connection. Awareness is the first step toward addressing these challenges.

2. Communication: Talk openly about the impact of routine and stress on

your relationship. Mutual understanding creates a foundation for finding solutions.

3. Shared Goals: Set shared goals to manage routine and stress together, fostering a sense of unity in facing life's demands.

Maintaining Closeness Amidst Busyness

Maintaining closeness requires intention, especially when schedules become hectic. Prioritizing your relationship, even during demanding times, strengthens the bond you share.

Strategies for Closeness:

1. Quality Over Quantity: Focus on the quality of interactions rather than their quantity. Make the most of the time you have together.

2. Micro-Connections: Create moments of connection even within the busiest days. A heartfelt text or a surprise gesture can bridge distances.

3. Scheduled Connection: Dedicate specific times for connecting, whether it's a morning coffee ritual or an evening catch-up session.

Reinventing Routine for Romance

Routine need not be an obstacle to romance; it can be a canvas upon which love is painted. By infusing intention and creativity, routine can become an ally in nurturing your connection.

Romanticizing Routine:

1. Shared Rituals: Develop routines that are meaningful to both of you, such as cooking together or unwinding with a shared activity.

2. Spontaneous Surprises: Surprise your partner with spontaneous acts of affection within your routine, such as leaving notes or planning surprise dates.

3. Open Communication: Continuously communicate about what you both need to keep the relationship thriving within the structure of routine.

The Transformative Power of Adaptability

The key to maintaining romance amidst routine and stress lies in adaptability. Partners must be willing to adjust their approach and actively seek solutions to overcome these challenges.

Embracing Adaptability:

1. Shared Strategies: Collaborate on strategies to tackle routine and stress as a team. Joint efforts foster a sense of unity and shared responsibility.

2. Flexibility: Be willing to adjust plans and expectations when routine and stress disrupt your original intentions.

3. Celebrate Small Victories: Celebrate the victories, no matter how small, that you achieve in maintaining closeness despite life's demands.

Love's Resilience: A Testimony of Time

The endurance of love is evident in its ability to weather routine and stress. When partners navigate these challenges together, they not only deepen their connection but also create a legacy of resilience that stands as a testament to their enduring bond.

Through the pages of this chapter, let the wisdom of overcoming routine and stress guide your journey. By employing strategies that prioritize communication, adaptability, and connection, you'll discover that even amidst life's demands, your love story continues to unfold with unwavering strength and unwavering devotion.

11

Rediscovering Self and Partner

In the embrace of a relationship, the journey of self-discovery and personal growth continues. This chapter delves into the profound significance of encouraging individuality within the union, celebrating both your own self and your partner's unique aspirations. It explores the art of nurturing self-discovery and fostering unwavering support, creating a space where the relationship and personal growth harmoniously intertwine.

The Symphony of Individual Growth

Personal growth is a symphony that plays throughout life. In a relationship, it harmonizes with the shared journey, enhancing the bond by allowing each partner to flourish individually.

Nurturing Self-Discovery:

1. Passion Pursuit: Encourage your partner to pursue their passions and interests, providing the space and support for them to delve into what ignites their soul.

2. Constant Evolution: Understand that growth is a continuous process. Embrace the evolution of your partner's interests, goals, and identity.

3. Shared Learning: Embark on new experiences together, allowing both partners to learn and evolve side by side.

Celebrating Your Partner's Individuality

In celebrating your partner's individuality, you validate their uniqueness and create an environment where they feel truly seen and appreciated.

Honoring Aspirations:

1. Active Listening: Engage in open conversations about your partner's dreams and aspirations. Show genuine interest and support.

2. Shared Excitement: Celebrate your partner's achievements and milestones as if they were your own, expressing pride and enthusiasm.

3. Respect for Choices: Respect your partner's decisions, even if they differ from your own preferences. Trust their judgment and autonomy.

Fostering Unwavering Support

Support is the backbone that carries the weight of dreams. By fostering an environment of unwavering support, partners become each other's cheerleaders in the journey of self-discovery.

Principles of Support:

1. Empathy: Put yourself in your partner's shoes, understanding their feelings and challenges as they pursue their aspirations.

2. Encouragement: Offer words of encouragement, reminding your partner that you believe in their potential and capacity for success.

3. Shared Efforts: Collaborate on projects, endeavors, and challenges, working together to achieve common goals while also nurturing individual growth.

The Tapestry of Shared Growth

The journey of rediscovering self and partner is not one of separation but of unity. Partners grow as individuals, yet their growth intertwines to create a rich tapestry of shared experiences, mutual respect, and unwavering love.

Balancing Individuality and Togetherness:

1. Shared Reflection: Regularly reflect on your individual growth and how it contributes to the growth of the relationship as a whole.

2. Communication: Continuously communicate about your individual aspirations, goals, and how you envision your partner's role in your journey.

3. Adaptable Bonds: Understand that as you both evolve individually, your relationship evolves as well. Embrace the adaptability of your bond.

Cherishing the Journey of Self and Partner

In nurturing self-discovery and supporting individual aspirations, partners sow the seeds of mutual growth and shared fulfillment. By celebrating each other's uniqueness and creating a space for personal evolution, the relationship becomes a vessel for continuous exploration, personal expansion, and the rich joys of discovering oneself and each other anew.

As you journey through this chapter, let the wisdom of embracing individuality and supporting aspirations guide your path. By fostering an environment of growth, you'll witness the love between you and your partner flourish as you each unfurl the vibrant petals of your individual selves within the radiant garden of your shared connection.

12

Sustaining a Lifelong Journey of Romance

As you stand on the threshold of this chapter, it's a moment to reflect on the remarkable journey you've undertaken in rediscovering romance. The path you've traversed has been one of growth, connection, and shared experiences. This chapter delves into the art of sustaining this journey—a lifelong commitment to keeping the flame alive, the love vibrant, and the relationship an enduring source of joy and fulfillment.

Reflecting on the Progress

Take a moment to acknowledge the progress you've made. Reflect on the transformation that has taken place—from rediscovering passion to fostering individual growth within the relationship. Celebrate the moments of connection, the laughter shared, and the challenges faced together.

Celebrate Achievements:

1. Journaling: Consider maintaining a journal where you chronicle the milestones, breakthroughs, and moments of love that have defined your journey.

2. Shared Reflection: Set aside time to reflect together on how far you've come and the love that continues to grow.

3. Express Gratitude: Express gratitude for your partner's efforts and the journey you've undertaken together.

Embracing Ongoing Efforts

Sustaining the journey of romance requires a commitment to ongoing effort. It's about continuously nurturing the connection and adapting to the changing tides of life.

Efforts for Sustained Romance:

1. Adaptable Approach: Understand that the strategies that worked in the past may need adjustment as you both evolve.

2. Regular Check-Ins: Make it a practice to have regular conversations about the state of your relationship and any adjustments needed.

3. Shared Goals: Set joint goals for the future, whether they involve travel, personal accomplishments, or further deepening your connection.

Creating a Tapestry of Enduring Love

Your journey is not one of finality, but a perpetually evolving tapestry of love that continues to weave its magic through the seasons of life.

Continuity in Motion:

1. Innovation: Embrace innovation in your relationship. Be open to new ideas, experiences, and ways to show love.

2. Adventures Together: Continue to explore new activities and embark on adventures to keep the excitement alive.

3. Weathering Challenges: Understand that challenges are a natural part of any journey. Face them as a united front, knowing that your bond is resilient.

Legacy of Love

Sustaining a lifelong journey of romance is a legacy you'll leave behind. It's the testament to your dedication, the narrative of your enduring love story that future generations will marvel at.

Fostering a Legacy:

1. Inspiration to Others: Your commitment to love can inspire others in their own journey of rediscovering romance.

2. Leading by Example: Lead by example, showing that love is a continuous journey that requires effort, care, and adaptability.

3. Lifetime of Memories: The memories you create along the way become the tapestry of your love, to be cherished for generations.

Embracing Forever Love

As you close this chapter, remember that the journey you've embarked upon is not confined to pages—it's an infinite story that will continue to be written with every passing day. Embrace the joys, challenges, and the extraordinary privilege of loving and being loved. The journey of sustaining a lifelong romance is not a destination; it's an ongoing celebration of the timeless, forever love that binds you and your partner, weaving a legacy of connection and devotion that transcends the bounds of time itself.

Conclusion: Embracing the Journey of Rediscovering Romance

As we reach the final chapter of this journey, it's an opportune moment to reflect on the transformative path you've traversed—the path of rediscovering romance, deepening connections, and fostering enduring love. The pages you've turned have revealed a tapestry of wisdom, insights, and strategies that have illuminated the way toward a more vibrant and fulfilling romantic relationship. As you take a moment to pause and reflect, let's encapsulate the key lessons and takeaways that have emerged from this profound exploration.

Lesson 1: Romance is an Evolution

Romance is not a static entity; it's a living, breathing force that evolves with time. From the initial sparks of attraction to the seasoned depths of connection, your relationship's journey is marked by growth and transformation.

Lesson 2: Intention is the Catalyst

Intention is the spark that ignites the flame of rediscovered romance. By choosing to prioritize and invest in your relationship, you create the foundation for enduring passion and connection.

Lesson 3: Communication is Key

Open and honest communication is the bridge that connects hearts. Deep conversations, active listening, and vulnerability form the cornerstone of a relationship that flourishes.

Lesson 4: Novelty Nurtures Passion

Novelty infuses life into the everyday, fostering passion and excitement. Whether through new experiences, surprise gestures, or spontaneous adventures, infusing your relationship with novelty reignites the spark.

Lesson 5: Individuality and Unity Coexist

The journey of self-discovery within a relationship enhances both individual growth and shared connection. Celebrating each other's uniqueness and supporting individual aspirations creates a harmonious dance of unity and diversity.

Lesson 6: Love is an Ongoing Journey

Love isn't a destination—it's a lifelong journey of commitment, growth, and devotion. Sustaining romance requires ongoing effort, adaptability, and a willingness to embrace change.

Takeaway: Rediscover, Revitalize, Reconnect

As you close this chapter and carry these lessons and takeaways forward, let them serve as guiding stars in your relationship's journey. Continuously rediscover the magic that drew you together, revitalize your connection through intentional efforts, and reconnect on a deep and enduring level.

The Call to Action: A Love That Lasts

In a world filled with distractions and demands, the choice to nurture your romantic connection is a powerful act of love. It's a commitment to cultivate a love that stands the test of time, one that grows richer with every shared moment, every whispered secret, and every shared dream.

A Final Note of Inspiration:

May your journey of rediscovering romance be one that unfolds through the tapestry of your days, weaving a narrative of enduring passion and connection. As you embrace the lessons learned, remember that the love you nurture today has the power to shape not only your story but also the legacy of love you leave behind. Your journey is a testament to the incredible capacity of the human heart—to love, to endure, and to forever rediscover the profound magic of romance.

www.ingramcontent.com/pod-product-compliance
Lightning Source LLC
LaVergne TN
LVHW012131070526
838202LV00056B/5946